Why Are You Barefoot?

DR. JEFF BRODSKY

Archway Publishing books may be ordered through booksellers or by contacting:

Archway Publishing
1663 Liberty Drive
Bloomington, IN 47403
www.archwaypublishing.com
1 (888) 242-5904

Because of the dynamic nature of the Internet, any web addresses or links contained in
this book may have changed since publication and may no longer be valid. The views
expressed in this work are solely those of the author and do not necessarily reflect the views
of the publisher, and the publisher hereby disclaims any responsibility for them.

Any people depicted in stock imagery provided by Getty Images are models,
and such images are being used for illustrative purposes only.
Certain stock imagery © Getty Images.

ISBN: 978-1-4808-6609-6 (sc)
ISBN: 978-1-4808-6610-2 (hc)
ISBN: 978-1-4808-6608-9 (e)

This book is a work of non-fiction. Unless otherwise noted, the author and the publisher make
no explicit guarantees as to the accuracy of the information contained in this book and in
some cases, names of people and places have been altered to protect their privacy.

Print information available on the last page.

Archway Publishing rev. date: 1/21/2019

I am dedicating this book to all the children, teens and young women who are still crying out to be rescued and long for their freedom – this book is for you.

I am also dedicating the book to a very special young girl in Anchorage, Alaska. In 2016, when Braelynn Hufford was only 8 years old, she taught me that even a young child can make a difference in the fight against child slavery, when she took it upon herself to bake peanut flavored dog biscuits and sell them to raise money for the Alaska Barefoot Mile. I was astounded when she raised over $1,000. She's a true inspiration.

I also give a special dedication to my 6 grandchildren: Izac, Emma, Leah, Malakai, Asher and Izzy. When I think of each of you, I am motivated to action in the work God has called me to do, in the rescue of children all over the world, who do not know the freedom that each of you have. I am a blessed man having each of you in my life. The greatest sound to my ears is when I hear you call me "Papa!"

A very heartfelt dedication is made posthumously to Andrew Pepperd who sadly died with his father Josh in a helicopter accident. Andrew loved the ministry of JOY International and worked our booth at The Alaska Barefoot Mile in Anchorage selling bracelets made by rescued girls in Cambodia. For the rest of my life, I will always remember the excitement and sheer joy he showed when after selling a bracelet he would enthusiastically proclaim, "I just sold another bracelet!" Andrew and his Dad will always hold a special place in my heart.

This book would not be in your hands without the following people in my life. Always first and foremost is my precious wife and life partner of 43 years, Gail. Without question, My Love, you are my greatest blessing. My children: Jeni, Lance and Meghan – you bring me immeasurable joy and constant inspiration. Naomi Woo – I've watched you grow from a little girl to a beautiful, magnificent woman of God. Thanks for the invitation to speak at Front Range Christian School which was the catalyst for this book. Thanks also for leading the teams to Cambodia. It wouldn't happen without you! Finally, I could not do this book without the input from two of my incredible staff of Gina Moran and Alyssa McKinley. I cannot thank God enough for bringing them into my life and the work of JOY International!

"Who's ready for our special speaker today?" my teacher, Miss Porter, asked. The boy across from me rolled his eyes. But then she caught our attention when she said, "This will sound a little strange, but the man coming to speak today has been BAREFOOT since 2010!"

"Seriously?" I thought, "He's been barefoot for so many years? How is that possible? Maybe THIS was one speaker who wouldn't be boring."

I raised my hand. "Yes Emma?" Miss Porter asked.

"Miss Porter, does he go barefoot all the time, even here in Colorado? Even in the winter? Even in the snow?"

Miss Porter laughed and said, "Emma, why don't you ask him when he gets here? I'm sure he would be happy to answer any questions." Then she had us all go to the auditorium. All the other classes were there too.

When the speaker walked in, I laughed because he looked just like Santa Claus! He had a white beard, curly hair, round glasses and rosy cheeks! But you could see that everyone was looking at his feet to see if he was really barefoot. Me too! Yep! Omigosh! He really was BAREFOOT! Miss Porter wasn't kidding!

"Alright everybody," she said, "let's welcome our special guest speaker today, the president and founder of JOY International, Dr. Jeff Brodsky." We clapped loudly as he walked on the stage with a big smile.

"Good morning boys and girls!" he greeted us. "Hey, how come everybody's looking at me funny? I know; it's because you think I'm Santa Claus, right? No? Then what is it? Is something wrong?" Lots of kids started laughing and shouting out,

"Yeah! You're barefoot! Where are your shoes and socks?"

"Oh, so that's it, huh? Well, I'm sure you're all wondering why I'm barefoot. Well, there's a good reason, and I promise that's something I'll share a little later with you, okay?

"Right now, I have a very important question to ask you. Are you ready? Here goes: If your mother sold you, would she be a good mom or a bad mom?"

"Huh?" I thought. "What'd he say? Is this a trick question?"

"Let me ask you again," he said. "If your mother sold you to someone, would she be a good mom or a bad mom?"

"Bad!" everyone said, "Really bad!"

"She'd be an awful mom!" one boy yelled out.

"Of course, that would be terrible if my mom sold me." I thought, "Are you kidding me? No way! It would be horrible! Why would any mother ever, ever sell their child? That could NEVER be good. Could it?"

After it got quiet, Dr. Jeff said, "I'm going to need some volunteers. Who would like to come up here and help me?"

Everybody in the room raised their hands. Omigosh, I thought my hand was going to fall off because I was waving it as hard as I could! "Please pick me, please, please, PLEASE pick me!" I prayed.

Dr. Jeff walked around the room, and he chose five kids from all different grades. "I need just one more volunteer," he said, walking over to our 6th grade class.

"Oh God, please let him pick me!" I was praying, "Oh please, please pick me Dr. Jeff!"

As he walked around looking at the kids in my class, he turned and then he looked right at me and said, "Hi, what's your name?"

"Emma!" I said.

"Hi Emma, how about you?"

Omigosh, I was so excited, I could hardly stand it, but, I must admit, I was a little nervous too. As he reached out for my hand and led me to the stage with the other children, I wondered; "What's he gonna do with us?"

Then Dr. Jeff asked Mr. Sheldon, the fifth-grade teacher, and my teacher, Miss Porter, to come up. Mr. Sheldon's face got a little red when Dr. Jeff said they would be the pretend mom and dad. Everybody laughed. He also picked Mr. Keller and asked him to stand on the side until he called him over.

Dr. Jeff lined us up according to size. I was the next to tallest. "Okay everybody," he said, "as you know, there are many nations in the world. Well, we are going to visit one of them right now. It's called the imagi-nation."

"Wow! That's so cool!" I thought.

"I want you to imagine that Mr. Sheldon and Miss Porter are married, and these are their children." That caused a lot of giggles.

Then Dr. Jeff shared the following story:

"Mr. Sheldon lives in a very poor country with his family. He can't find a job, and they have no money. Mr. Sheldon is so desperate that he goes into the street every day begging people for money, so he can buy food for his family. But it's just not enough, and the children are very hungry. Sometimes all they have is just enough money for some rice."

I felt my stomach tighten at the thought of being that hungry.

"The family also has no place to live, so they all have to live in the street. The father is very sad because he sees his children go hungry every day.

"One day, Mr. Sheldon wakes up early in the morning and goes out begging. After many hours, he doesn't even have enough money for a bag of rice. He doesn't know what else to do. Instead of going back to his family, he leaves them. He doesn't want to, but he thinks that if he does leave, then there would be one less person that needs food. His wife and children never see him again."

All the kids were very quiet.

Dr. Jeff then had Mr. Sheldon step down from the stage. When he walked past me, I could see that Mr. Sheldon looked very sad.

"After a couple of days," Dr. Jeff continued, "the mother became desperate! She didn't know what happened to her husband, and with him gone, she didn't know how she could possibly feed her children. Without money to buy food, her children would starve! She took them to the streets and told them all to beg for money."

Dr. Jeff then motioned for Mr. Keller to come stand next to him, and he whispered something in Mr. Keller's ear. Mr. Keller spoke to Miss Porter in a voice that sounded very strange; a shiver ran down my back.

"Hi Miss," he said, "I see you're asking people for money. That's so sad that you have to do that. Are all these children yours?"

"Yes, they are my children," Miss Porter nodded her head. "My husband is gone, and we have nothing. We need money for food."

"I have an idea that might help you and your children," Mr. Keller said. "I live in a very big house, and I have a cook and a gardener, and they could use some help. I could give you some money in exchange for one of your girls." Miss Porter frowned at him.

"She can come work for me. She can help my cook or gardener, and I'll pay her, so she can give money back to you every week. Plus, I'll help her learn a good trade, so she can get a great job when she's older. I'll pay for her to go to school for a few hours a day. She can even come and see you once in a while."

Dr. Jeff whispered in Mr. Keller's ear again, and then Mr. Keller said, "How about if I give you $50 for her?" Mr. Keller then looked at all the children standing there next to Miss Porter. Then he pointed at me and said, "How about her?" I don't know why, but I started shaking.

Then Dr. Jeff turned to all the students and said, "Boys and girls, when a mother like this needs money for food for all her children, and someone comes along and offers her $50, it can be a lot of money to that mom. In very poor countries, that much money can feed her and all her children for a few months.

"'If I sell one child to this man,' the mother thinks, 'she will live in a nice house, have a bed to sleep in, have plenty of food to eat, a chance for a good job, and she'll get an education. She'll even make enough money to help us, and I can get more food for the rest of the family. I would have one less mouth to feed, plus I can still see her once in a while. This will be a blessing!'"

Miss Porter knew what Dr. Jeff was trying to teach everyone, so she looked at Mr. Keller and said, "Yes. I will do this. I will sell my daughter to you."

Mr. Keller pretended to give money to Miss Porter, and he took my hand and gently pulled me closer to him. I stood by his side. Miss Porter began to cry. I don't know why, but so did I.

Dr. Jeff had Miss Porter and the other children leave the stage. All that was left was Mr. Keller, Dr. Jeff and me up there. Dr. Jeff turned to all the students and said, "There's something important you need to know. Mr. Keller is a liar. He wasn't telling the truth. He doesn't have a big house. He doesn't have a cook or a gardener. If this really happened, Emma would never see her mother, brothers, or sisters again. He would make her into a slave and make her do very bad things. If she didn't do what she was told, she would be beaten every day until she obeyed him. Although we were just pretending, sadly, this happens every day to children all over our world."

Dr. Jeff whispered something else in Mr. Keller's ear. Mr. Keller then asked me for my shoes and socks. I didn't understand why, but I took them off and gave them to him. Dr. Jeff told everyone that Mr. Keller did that because now it would be harder for me to run away.

Then he said to Mr. Keller, "Thank you very much for playing our bad guy." Mr. Keller handed me my shoes and socks and sat down.

Now Dr. Jeff and I were both standing on the stage alone and barefoot.

Dr. Jeff looked out at everyone and said, "Let me ask you again the first question I asked; Do you think that the mother sold her child because she was a good mom or a bad mom? Do you think she loves her child?" I could see all the kids nodding their heads yes.

Dr. Jeff showed us how even a good mom, a mom who really loves her child, could sell her because she really believes she is doing the right thing.

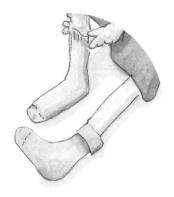

"Alright everybody, we were using our imagination today, but like I said, this really happens, every day, all over the world. There are many bad people who will lie to innocent, hurting people so that they can steal their children and make them into slaves. That is why I am barefoot, boys and girls - to remind myself every day that there are millions of children who are being held and used as slaves.

"One day I was in a very poor country, and I saw many children living in a garbage dump with no shoes. After seeing these children who were all barefoot, I wondered; 'What would it be like to live barefoot every day?' That night, I took off my shoes and socks, and I have been barefoot ever since. Do I like being barefoot? NO! Living in the mountains of Colorado, it can get very COLD in the winter! Being barefoot reminds me that there are desperate children, and it helps me show others that there are children who are forced to be slaves all over the world. These children need our help. They need someone to rescue them."

It was very quiet in the auditorium, except for the sound of lots of children taking off their shoes and socks. It was really amazing to watch as I stood barefoot on the stage with Dr. Jeff.

"The story doesn't end here my young friends!" Dr. Jeff continued, "I work for an organization called JOY International, and this is the work we do. We rescue children who are sold into slavery!" He lifted my hand and said, "My job is to find children like Emma who were either sold or kidnapped and forced to be slaves. Our rescue teams do whatever they can to get them out and into a safe place and hopefully back to their families!

"Every child deserves to have hope for the future and a life filled with true joy. Every child should have a chance to be happy and safe, just like you."

Dr. Jeff gave me a hug and thanked me for helping him, and I went back to my seat. There was so much going through my mind as I thought about everything that he told us. There are so many children who need our help.

Then our principal, Mr. Johnson, got up on the stage, and we all laughed and clapped when we saw that he was barefoot too! He said something that surprised and excited everyone; "Dr. Jeff has a very important job, and he could use our help. Would you like to help him?"

"YES!" everyone yelled out.

"I had an idea when I saw some of you taking off your shoes and socks," he said. "Would anyone like to be barefoot in school?"

Omigosh! Everyone started taking off their shoes!

"Wait a minute!" Mr. Johnson said, "Not yet! We will send you home with a permission slip to your parents. If you have it signed, you can go barefoot in school for 3 days. You will have an opportunity to get your friends, neighbors, and relatives to sponsor you. You can ask them to help you by contributing $1 or more, per day. Then, when the 3 days are over, we'll give all the money we collect to JOY International to help Dr. Jeff rescue more children. How does that sound?"

WOW! Everybody was cheering!

Mr. Johnson thanked Dr. Jeff for coming to our school and teaching us such an important lesson.

Later in the afternoon, my mom picked me up and asked, "So how was school today?"

"Mom, I have to tell you what we learned... we had an awesome speaker! He shared something I'll never forget. His name was Dr. Jeff, and he told us about children, and then when I was sold...and Mom, can you help me make a lemonade stand to help..." Before I could finish telling her, she interrupted me, shouting,

"Emma what do you mean you were sold? Where are your shoes? Why are you barefoot?"

I hugged her really tight and said, "Mom, thanks for loving me!"

ATTENTION PARENTS:

There are many things I could have shared in the book about ways to both inform and protect your children. This being a book for your children, due to the sensitive nature of much of that material, I simply could not put these in the book for reasons I'm sure you can understand. If you would like information on ways to both inform and protect your children, please visit www.joy.org/parents.

How You and Your Family Can Get Involved

Here is a List of ways you can help stop child Slavery with your children
Special thanks to **Diana Scimone** and **The Born2Fly Project (www.born2fly.org)**

1. **Go** to the JOY International website and become a **JOY FREEDOM PARTNER!** At the website we have a page with many ideas for fundraising projects you can do with your children.

2. **Research** abolitionists and discuss this with your child. Learn about some of the historical abolitionists like Harriet Tubman, Frederick Douglass, Harriet Beecher Stowe, Abraham Lincoln, William Wilberforce and many others. See if there is an abolitionist group in your city, and if there isn't one, start one!

3. **Learn how to make Survival Bracelets**. One 12-year-old girl, after hearing Dr. Jeff speak, made 100 bracelets and sold them for $10 each. She raised $1,200 for JOY International.

4. **Host** a party and make anti-slavery t-shirts to wear. Come up with creative sayings and designs. You can have a 3rd World Meal – Check with our office for information.

5. **Give** a gift in someone's honor. Donate to an organization, like JOY International, in his or her name.

6. **Introduce** JOY International to a foundation or corporation. Many times a company or business or even an individual will do matching funds. Check to see if the company you work for does this for its employees.

7. **Invite** Dr. Jeff Brodsky to share about the work of JOY International at your church or school.

8. **Host** or participate in a **Barefoot Mile** to raise awareness and funds for JOY International. Learn more at www.joy.org.

9. **Write to** your legislators and ask what they're doing to stop the slavery.

10. **Forgo** birthday or Christmas presents: Instead ask family and friends to donate to JOY International in your name.

11. **Pray** for the rescue work of JOY International!

12. **Organize** a fund-raising party for JOY International: Contact our office for help.

13. **Go** to http://productsofslavery.org - This is a phenomenal interactive map showing countries and products using children and forced labor.

Quotes

"You may choose to look the other way, but you can never say again that you did not know." ~ William Wilberforce

"If slavery is not wrong, nothing is wrong." ~ Abraham Lincoln

"How wonderful it is that nobody need wait a single moment before starting to improve the world." ~ Anne Frank

"The world is a dangerous place to live; not because of the people who are evil, but because of the people who don't do anything about it." ~ Albert Einstein

"You must be the change you wish to see in the world." ~ Gandhi

"The only thing necessary for the triumph of evil is for good men to do nothing." ~ Sir Edmund Burke

"A hundred years from now it will not matter what my bank account was, the sort of house I lived in, or the kind of car I drove...but the world may be a better place because I was important in the life of a child." ~ Dr. Forest E. Whitcraft

"Awareness without action is apathy." ~ Dr. Jeff Brodsky

JOY INTERNATIONAL IS DEDICATED TO THE
RESCUE, RESTORATION, AND REINTEGRATION
OF CHILDREN, TEENS AND YOUNG WOMEN
AFFECTED BY TRAFFICKING AND THE PREVENTION
OF CHILD TRAFFICKING WORLDWIDE.

Learn more about our work at: www.joy.org

JOY International
PO BOX 571
Conifer, CO 80433

Printed in the United States
By Bookmasters